Love & Purgatory

Poetry from an Unstable Mind

Genevieve Kinslow

authorHOUSE®

AuthorHouse™
1663 Liberty Drive
Bloomington, IN 47403
www.authorhouse.com
Phone: 833-262-8899

Published by AuthorHouse 03/23/2023

ISBN: 979-8-8230-0438-1 (sc)
ISBN: 979-8-8230-0437-4 (hc)
ISBN: 979-8-8230-0436-7 (e)

Library of Congress Control Number: 2023905403

To Felicia,
thank you for everything

Contents

Prologue

I wrote my first book at age fifteen, it ate me from the inside out until I was forced to expel it. I am enthralled with, and quite married to, horror, but to confine myself to one genre would be to define myself - which I ultimately conclude to be the same as living as an immutable and boring bolder (unwittingly free of spray paint).

My obsession ranges as far as my interests; death, life, hate, love, disgusting and vile imagery, and beautifully eloquently designed phrases. To be one thing often despises pre-existing or soon to be lived in contradictions.

Who hasn't written a poetry book? It's supposedly easy and makes an easy buck. If your name proceeds your character, why not cash in that fame in simple anecdotes you wrote in the shower?

"My poetry is different" is a self-centered ideology, and selfishness is not in my nature (as long as I continue to change it), but often enough difference is obscene and freakish enough to stand alone (be cornered). My words hold meaning I must to show others, not in the way of taking off my clothes but rather tear away my skin; opening my chest cavity for anyone who wishes to observe.

Art should be consumed, tasted, and digested. My prerogative is to be eaten, don't you be a voyeur but rather a participant. So consume me, and let something be gained from my internal torment and any pretty words that may spill while I am being feasted upon.

This collection varies from self inflicted love letters, to the worst pain I willingly ingested, and festered. There are narrative stories, personal incriminations, things stuck in between, and sometimes neither existing or feasible. You may guess if they happened to me truthfully, or perhaps they're all lies;

Either way, please enjoy me.

A Life I Wasn't Supposed To Keep

I was supposed to die
So breathing is still very strange
Exhalations are always followed by inhalations, it's
unfamiliar to feel security in that
I shouldn't be here
I was never supposed to live this long

My name was written next to a time that has long since
passed
A dedicated history of end dates, the punctuation of fates
My own I have managed to escape
But why me?
Just because I fought with everything I have, and everything
I've never had?

Why am I alive?
Why do I get a second chance?
Could I possibly be that important?
I don't really think so
And I'm not really that thankful
But I am here, and that's far more than enough

So for now, I guess I'll keep myself alive.

Afterlife

After I was decapitated - I woke up.
The pain a phantom, which led me to believe that I was as
well.

I reach out to my lover, but I reach right through their face.
I can pull my head off my body, my neck nothing more than
a table for my face to sit upon.

Eternity waits patently for my eventual mental snap,
Which indeed is evident.

Walking cold halls of a house, I only knew as warm,
Drowns me in the air you breath through my apparition,
It's suddenly suffocating and pouring into your lungs as if
it were a liquid.

I only know alone.
I only understand my current, the past a distant dream.

I live inside each and every second, who's length is no less
than a year.
And I watch dust settle, as I move slower.

Death is not scary, nor should it intimidate.
Dying is the easy part.

It's living afterwards, lost in perpetual nothing, that should
be feared.

AHHH

I have let myself get in my own way for my entire life.
I allowed pain to cloud my inner judgment, and I let my creativity soak when it should have burned me from the inside out.

But it all got so tiring, always feeling so bad for myself, always feeling so terrible.
There was objects of my affection of which I could have turned to, but I starved myself of them too.
Why would anything be so gracious as to allow me to enjoy it peacefully?
Silly self deprecating thoughts, plague me like an illness and eat my insides, won't you?

I've wasted so much time.
The years I spent pooling over myself, laying on my bed and staring at the ceiling like I was spiting some god.

I could have been writing for so long.
Those days I did nothing but cry, break down, hurt;
I could have been spilling the overflowing stories in my brain, yet I let them sink and choke under my own suffocation orders.

Alone With You

Alone is something I am used to,
It's something I thrive on.
Social execution becomes so tiring after so little.
But being alone with you,
Is nothing like I've experienced before.

Alone I am free to be anything my mind wishes.
I may scream on my own, sing, dance, and cry.
Of my own prerogative, I am allowed myself.
I've never been able to be like that, not alone.

Alone can be between two people.
Alone together.
I've never understood anything that makes sense resolving
that idea.
But I understand it thoroughly now.

I don't how I didn't see it earlier.
But I also absolutely do.
Comfortable isn't something you think about, it just exists.
We know anxiety like we know the friend who just keeps
talking and will follow you until you can escape.
But alone with you, anxiety only appears in elation,
Or maybe hysteria is more accurate.

Alone Without You

Having never slept in someone's arms before
I didn't know it would be so easy
Or that I could get that used to it

With your arms around me
No nightmares overtake me
When you kiss me, no bad dreams come to plague me

I thought falling asleep without you would be hard
And it is
But waking up alone, with only the memory of you, is hell
all over again.

Am I Lonely?

I'm not sure I feel so lonely
Once again I'm surrounded by people
But I don't feel that normal lonely

The type you get in a crowd
Everyone swarming in and out like a mess of a mass
And you stand in the middle and are entirely ignored

But here I am
Speaking to people, and them speaking back to me
It's so very strange, I'm not sure I'll get used to it

It used to be so easy to disappear
Fade into the back of the crowd, hide behind the tall people
in pictures
But now I'm in the front, and I am no longer ignored

And the weirdest part
Is that normal to me is to be ridiculed, ignored, and shamed
for my person
But now I am celebrated, and it's a divinity I never thought
I'd be allowed to taste.

So why do I feel like I should still be outcasted?

(No such thing as) Bad Poetry

Normally, you're so sure of everything,
All it took was for me to stop laughing
And you were squirming.
I used to attentively praise you
For your wit, as well as your flaws.
But when I used my influence,
Not sucking you off for five seconds,
You set fires kindled out of anxiety.

It didn't have to end like this.
In a parallel, some window in the distance, I see us
Happy.
I see us together.
But in this shattered existence,
You were too scared to stop the punch.

Hit me and revive,
The boredom in your chest drains us all through a straw.
A slow consumption,
A sandy ache against our skin,
Make it painful -
Make it fun.
Tear me open and play around with my insides;
Use your teeth, a fork, a shovel,
I don't care.
Just postpone my boredom already.

Bathroom Anxiety

Oh how you smite me,
The open window who watches me across the bathroom
laughed at my despair.

No curtains hide my figure,
I'm my haste I did not notice.
Mindfulness could have prevented it had I not had a
beautiful woman,
With only a room between us,
Waiting in my bed.

But If my neighbor,
The one with the binoculars,
Who sometimes watches my mother,
Was so included to be a voyeur right then-
I'd have no way of knowing,
For the sun had set three hours ago.

He could see me in my vulnerability,
If he is so pleased, in that moment.

My reflection looks back at me,
Shame bores fire within a mirrored iris that cannot keep
contact with its twin.

I hadn't even finished when I noticed it either,
I ran inside the room,
I was mostly done,
Then I looked to my right:

And of course, I'm changing my underwear.

Blind to the Irony

Can't you see
That everything you did to us
Is what's happening to you?

"It's so unfair!"

Yes, yes it is.
And we had to deal with it for months.
We had to cry so many nights
In anguish, in frustration,
Because it was never fair for us.
And you didn't care, not at any point.

You've dealt with a fraction of it,
And you can't take it.

Our love was the collision of planets,
And you wouldn't allow us to watch the stars,
Or be at peace,
Or feel the love we'd both been deprived of our whole fucking
lives.

You tried to stop two souls from finding their mates.

And you want to give up,
Because it's too hard for you,
But you still don't fucking get it.

You told us we couldn't love each other,
And we pretended for you,
We did everything to keep your feelings together,
While we fell apart.

I don't care if you love him,
Even if it ruined a friendship,
Because you've always,
And always will,
Mean more to me.

I gave everything to you,
We both did.
We had the love of a lifetime,
And we had to pretend it didn't exist.

Because it hurt you too much.

We'll, how's that for you?
Karmas a bitch,
But for once she's being nice to us.

But you're blind.
Irony is as complex as fucking rocket science,
And as simplistic as a brick to the face,
And you still won't just wake up and face the music.

What you did to us,
Was always going to come back to kick you in the ass.

So I don't care that this is hard for you.
You did far worse to us, and I know you'll never apologize.

So stay confused, stay naive,
Stay fucking blind to the irony screaming at your unlocked door.

Blood!Blood!Blood!

Never let yourself forget the color of your blood.
Not that fake shit in movies, or blood in general.
No, *your* blood.
Leaking from *your* skin,
Yours alone.

Never forget the taste of your blood.
Not anyone else's.
No, the blood you alone drip for the altar of your god,
The one who lives in the back of your throat,
Your own personal demon, who shares your name.

Never forget the feeling of what it is to bleed.
Not when the scars close, a reminder you can almost forget
the feeling of.
No, remember the slice.
Or remind yourself, to go ahead and open those useless
veins.
You're not special, your blood looks the same as everybody
else's.

Bracelet

I wear the planets on my wrist, just above my veins.
What is my skin but the galaxies habitat, my freckles and hair are the stars littered by a careless God.
Whispers inside me are unseen, unheard, only tasted; a cosmos of purple which sits just above my elbow.

What am I now but an endless stream, dripping into a still pool of insanity?
The last of my skin is flushed down the sink, the blood will take much longer to scrub out.
My bones have been grinded to dust by rotten teeth, and my planets sing praise for their release.

But without me they fall apart.
The string of them cannot stay together without a body.
Without me, they are nothing but ideas.

God's creations spite their father, asking to be free.
But costs apply to nature as naturally as humanity stole the concept;
Freedom from the plan, losing all you love, just to have a will of your own.

Breathing Down My Neck

I always thought the phrase would be an uncomfortable
feeling
But clearly whoever thought of it didn't think it could mean
something far better
Than uncomfortable
Than unpleasant or dangerous

When you breathe on my neck
When you hold me to your chest as we fall asleep

Your breathing on my neck is safety
It's love
Reality crashes down me like waves
And for once I am thankful for being swallowed whole

When you kiss me I know you love me
When you hold me I know I can be myself

I've never slept in another's arms before
I never knew how wonderful it was
I'd hold a pillow and pretend it was a lover
But only flesh, heat, and the breathing on my neck, let me
know it's all real.

Bullshit

A mind that's brave and unusual often seeks out what destroys it.

Though I love and I want to be better, I cannot help the simplicity of destruction. I would love to crash my teeth against a hammer, to shove a blade into my intestines, or to rip apart my skin and unleash sandpaper upon my flesh.

Should I seek refuge or shall I let my own mind loose on itself? For the depravity of pain and of it all.

I'd love to give myself up to the gods. Just to face them, and spit at their feet.

BUZZED

In a blur the days past as quickly as flies,
Buzzed, swarmed, bitten, and called to the lantern -
A beacon of relaxation -
Once we wake up we will escape the embryos as we always do.

Follow the group and swarm the face,
Crawl into my ears and pierce the drums with a sickening
buzz,
Then bite me until nothing lasts which is not bleeding
and raw.

The same insects which feasted upon my blood and my flesh
Now adventure to my exposed cavity,
Filling up my entrails and spitting on my insides -

I am nothing, but a feast.

Captive Cuisine

As you know it, and as you don't xx,

I've been a vegan for as long as I can remember. My parents enforced from the day I was born, until the day I decided I would continue the practice. I was brought up knowing the inhumane suffering of animals and how humans massacred the likes of them. You know this of course, as I'm sure you remember me telling you, but I'm just giving a reason for an out of reason - reason.

And, although I am severely devoted to being a vegan, and my whole life I have never even thought of not being one, I still cannot resist one thing. The succulence of meat. Whether it be boiling, baking, satayed, or even raw, the smell stains my head and drives me dizzy. Nothing grinds my teeth harder than the sweet sensation and aggression the infiltration that my quivering nostrils are forced to brings forth!

"Just once," I tell myself, "Just one little time and never again!" I repeat in my head as I go online, scouring sights I'd never let my mother walk in on me while looking at. The public eyes on me of this consumption after such devotion would horrendously shatter me. And of course, thanks to you, I already know the perfect place to meet my desires.

And one other thing.

It doesn't matter to me what type of meat I have, I just need it once. It goes against everything I've ever valued, but just once couldn't hurt much, could it? And besides, what other meat would be so satisfying besides the very best your beautiful chef's have to offer!

There's already an overpopulation of animals, all be it our fault for that. So what's to happen to all of the corpses left behind? If the whole world was to turn vegan in a day, what would come of the remains of the animals so expertly raised.

If anything, I'm helping our economy.

That's why I'm here, of all places. I do not want any record of myself out in anywhere, stating that I made such consumption in such boldness.

And to you, I turn to my wonderful and most satisfactory supplier. For the many fumigated nights you have brought me, and such wonderful galaxies of stardust you have introduced me to. (And I know you run this little side business of yours). You've always treated me so well, given our past and all, so I put my trust in you. Just one little sample couldn't hurt, could it?

Not to mention, humans are the only animals that can consent, right?

Sincerely,
-You know who, in the now and in the how-

. ~*. ~ . ~ . * . ~ . ~ .*~ .

Dear valued customer,

Thank you for reaching out to my other branches of service. I have not let you down in the past with my other products, and I promise I won't let you down here.

If you want to continue our recent discussion on hallucinogenics, you know how to contact me.

As for my other business, here are my price listings:

Liver - $157,000
Heart - $119,00
Spleen - $533
Stomach - $508
Small Intestine - $2,519
Kidney - $262,000
Gallbladder - $1,219
Skin - $10 (per square inch)
Blood - $337 (per pints)
Skull (with teeth) - $1,200
Eyeballs - $1,525
Scalp - $602
Coronary Artery - $1,525
Shoulder - $500
Hand and forearm - $385

Thank you for your business, I hope we can satisfy your demands. If you have any complaints, or special instructions of the human you wish to consume, please list below in a follow up email.

And yes, as you've stated your concern in the past; all meat is collected from 'willing participants' and is treated with every sanitized precaution possible.

Regards,
Sawney-Bons distributions

Comfortably Naked

Exposed
That's how I should be
All around me only glimpse at my skin
May wonder what I look like under all the clothes I stole
from you

But for you
Just for you
As always
I will be exposed

You've pulled back my scalp already
And spooned through my brain long enough to understand
On a level that surpasses physical interaction

But there we are
And here I am
I'm definitely not ready
But I never will be

So expose me
And find what you'd like
Tie me down and explore
Take and do as you please

I'm terrified of you
But not your physical vessel
We know each other
Maybe too well

Now that we've collided
The universe will never be the same
And I don't want it any other way

Your hands
Your mouth
Your body
Has more worth to me than living

Expose me
And see what you want
You have my full consent to do with me as you please
So

Please.

Contemplation

It's okay to let your eyes linger on your scars
I've found it strange for a long time
Always expecting them to still be bleeding
Open and raw and bleeding
And bleeding
The blood running down my arm and into my mouth

But they're now just light little smiles
I hate that I did this to myself
And that's taken just as long to realize
I love and hate my scars

I'd always wished I'd made more
Even though there's not enough room on the canvas
Not even for a couple more brush strokes
But here I am
The warmth makes them shine again
And I find myself once more looking at them

Only now I just feel sad.

Contradiction

The burn of a kiss from a lover is sympathetic
To the delight of the embrace of a blade within a broken
surface

To be a contradiction is my choice
As much as it is my nature

The fault in being unpronounced
Is to always be unannounced

I want to string pretty words into rhythm and chaos
When I despise that beauty inside myself

To be one without the other
I am neither both nor in between

I am yes as equally as I am no
To be fluid is the blood that freezes in the heat of my
autocannibalism

I am everything due to nothing
And nothing derived from everything

Enjoy me, feast upon me, and digest enjoyment
And hate me as soil that is rotted with acidic pollution

My nature is virtuous and devious
I am not one without another

So find me solace in gratitude
And never let me sleep again.

Dainty Objects

A woman is asking for it if she wears provocative clothing.
I mean, she must be.
Why else would she put on those shorts,
Put on that shirt,
Wear those shoes.

Do you have a picture in your head?
Good.

Women ask to be assaulted by the clothing they wear.
They ask without words,
And they obviously mean "yes, more."
When they scream "please, stop."

No means yes when she wears slutty clothing.

Women are objects,
And they should be treated as such.
They don't have voices, nor do they have brains,
Definitely not thoughts of their own.

So use them, exploit them, destroy them.

It's never been vocalized, but it's what they all want.
Why else would they dress like that?
They're asking for it.

She wears a dress that shows her legs,
A shirt that outlines her body,

Shoes that make her walk funny.
She's asking for it.

Have I convince you yet?
That there's no exception to this rule?
Good.

Now ask again if she was asking for it:
If she's wearing overalls,
Her hair in short pigtails,
Clothes she wears to school.

And she's five years old.

But she must have been asking for it.
Otherwise, why would a man do such a thing?

It's so simple, really.
Just ask yourself this question,
And answer it even more easily:

"Because it was there."

Dinner Party

Little tiny feast,
I set the table with the whittled bones of previous dinners.
Did you enjoy the meal?
I know it's hard to speak;
All tied up,
And tied down to that chair.
Though I expect the hardest part about speech
Is the fact your mandible is missing.

Oh! But you look so good like that!
Your tongue flops out on your neck,
Only the gums attached to the top still remain.
Your teeth had to go first,
Don't you get it?

How else was I to bypass chewing?
You can't have your teeth,
That would disrespect my intentions.
You must swallow everything I give you.
I would prefer with a smile,
But I understand how your predicament could prevent that.

You were always supposed to be my guest,
You've always had a platecard and an assigned seat.
And I was pretty clear about when it started,
So why do you still scream?

You can't possibly form words, I made sure of that.
Gargles are more than enough for me to understand that
you're still hungry.
I just want to feed you,
Is that so much to ask?

But you let the food spill from your mouth.
I understand it's hard, I do,

I know you don't want to upset me.
But you can atleast put some fucking effort into it.

Disappointment

I picked up a house hold hammer.

It was at the 1889 Exposition Universelle, the date that marked the 100th anniversary of the French Revolution, that a great competition was launched in the Journal Officiel.

I opened my jaw as much as I could, slamming my teeth down to bite onto the metallic cheek.

The 1880s saw a time of booming architecture, none such as famous as the "Eiffel Tower."

The pain erupts like fire.

The eventual construction was never supposed to be permanent, and even though many citizens protested, it became a monument befitting france like a title.

I open my mouth, I push the hammer in further, and bite harder.

The first digging work started on the 26th January 1887. March 31st 1889, the Tower had been finished – 2 years, 2 months and 5 days.

I feel my teeth breaking, I force more of it down, the wood chipping and splintering.

During the time of building, however, the French residents who lived around the construction sight feared falling debris.

The metal head hits my gag reflex, and I drive the tool down my esophagus.

The Eiffel tower was made to be twice as sound as the original plans had described, the citizens using the excuse of instability to try and halt construction.

The claw digs into the back of my throat, and I pull it out slowly, before ramming it again harder.

It was the tallest building in the world, at the time of its construction, residents feared it would over shadow them.

My tastebuds erupt with the flavor of copper and metal, the burning pain finally consumes my mind.

Each of the 18,000 pieces used to construct the Tower were specifically designed and calculated, traced out to an accuracy of a tenth of a millimeter

I push the handle past my lips.

The heart of France, the great monument stood to defy any God who thought of striking her down, France had their symbol.

Standing still, my face is twisted upwards as the hammer stays in place, spearing my throat open wide.

"Likewise the many empty spaces built into the very elements of construction will clearly display the constant concern not to submit any unnecessary surfaces to the violent action of hurricanes, which could threaten the stability of the edifice" - Gustave Eiffel.

But that's disappointment, right? Because neither thing was a Candy Cane.

Disowned

There is only one thing that could ever make me believe in God.

Blasphemy is my kind, find me, and know me,
I will return.
Sulfur is the floor which I crawl on, and it burns me,
The air I breath scorches my insides, and I beg with bloody lips for more.
I belong at end of the rings, the bottom of the drain.

God, I spite you.
You're not real, what I went through wasn't holy.
But If this is your plan, then I know how it ends.
I know what I deserve, and I know what he does.
The one thing you never get wrong is justice for those who deserve it, those you've written to deserve it.

No devil in the great expanse of hell would do the job right.
God knows so.
The Devil's whispered this to me.
I am the sole being in any existence who is capable of torturing this man correctly.

Any form of compensation would start with solitary confinement.
Cage him for me, won't you?
I just know you will.
He will die soon, and I will live a long wonderful life without him.

I wake up every morning hoping each day is the day he dies,
Waiting for the creation of my new favorite holiday.

So hold him,
And wait for me to die.
Because I'm waiting, I will be waiting until sweet nothing
passes my cold lips.
I'm anxiously waiting to return to Hell,
It will be home to both of us, once again.

When I descend into hell,
On the wings of Satan,
I'm coming right for you.
The very first thing I'd do is rip your eyeballs out and force
you to chew on them.

You deserve all the hate I birthed to eat myself alive.
The pain I conjured, from your actions, should have always
been pointed and shot at you.
I am incapable of forgetting what you did, I am what I've
been through, I wish I could forget like you did.
And you don't know the half of it, you stop listening after "I."

We are destined.
You will be my captive, and I will be your God.
You will know submission.
You will know fear.
And you will understand what you've done to me.
And to her.
And her.

You'll understand.
When I get to flay you, I'll do so smiling.
Your vocal chords aren't need either, what a treat.
Nor your fingers, or toes, or hands, or feet, or arms, or legs.
No more testicles either!

You'll might understand, maybe when I'm done with you.
But we have eternity to get there.
You've taught me patience,
I'll wait my entire life for you to die,
For you to remorse, or repent.
I know patience like a scar knows serration.

And soon, you'll know everything I had to learn by myself,
And you'll never unlearn that lesson.
Just like me, your scars will tell a pitiful story.

Hopefully it's today.
Hopefully it's tomorrow.

All I know, all I am, is the one who was supposed to die-
But I survived.
I should have been the one to die first,
But that wouldn't be any fun at all.

I hope it's today.
I dream it's tomorrow.

We are no longer little girls with little worlds,
And no longer will little girls be censored of their little words.

Do something to me

Eat me alive, won't you?
Just fucking feast upon me. God, please.
The artist ability you uphold upon the sins of flesh, imposing upon upholstery, curtains, silhouetted by deeds of the past.
Eat me from the inside out.
I want you to reprimand me with your justice.
So unhinged, what really is right from wrong?
I no longer care about morality or it's angelic fracture over humanity, all I want is your finger to rip my skin with your nails.
Kill me, murder me, and maybe I shall find satisfaction.
Is this a love affair, a murder, or something better?

Why won't you just end me, already?
Thoughts parade inside me, raming into the walls of my subconscious until they turn red from the beatings.
Futility is but a dream, a reality and a curse I dream of sinking my teeth into.
I should be put away into a mental institute, where everything would make sense;
But free me, I beg fo you! I dream of freedom.
From myself, I wish of freedom, free from you and free from her.
Kill me before I must feel again.

What a matriarcal, a parental, imagery of a dove; the light snipping of easy bones, the head ripped from the body, a beautiful abscess so delicately decapitated, deliciously.
You, friend, know this.

So fucking end me already.

I beg of you.

I've been on my knees, and I shall return; if that is your wish of me.

Love doesn't describe my enquiry of the unfiltered requirement I seek: fucking kill me.

Buzzsaw, hammer, ax, hands around my throat, scalpel, poison or medication, any personal cause of death will do; or run me over with you car, whatever works.

Just do it already.

I just need you to do something, already.

Anything. Just. Do. Anything. To me.

You know I love to be teased, but I am no longer asking. I demand this from you. Chose my fate and make it happen. It doesn't have to be quick, it can be as slow as you want. Just fucking do something to me already.

Drunk Poetry

You sit across from me
Drawing a naked lady.

In the eyes of an art critic
Even they would come to tears.

Not from the beauty, she is quite present there,
But by the graceful and thoughtful touches.

Hands must have traced those curves,
Fingers delicately compose such exquisite lines.

Imagery of a goddess,
Created from the mind of an addict.

One so enraptured with the beauty of women,
It was so obvious how well she knew,
Just how beautiful the female figure really is.

Dry

I feel so dried out.

You know that feeling in the back of your throat after you've been crying?

That's where I am.

This morning I had something difficult to go through.

It was necessary to cry, other wise I would be forced into feeling nothing at all.

But this is better.

The roughness in my mouth and in my heart hurts like sandpaper on my skin.

But this is still better than feeling nothing at all.

Though I cried several times this morning, I still am consumed by this aching dryness which cannot be swept down by any rivers which I throw at it, hoping I'll just drown.

I am so terribly dried out.

It's not the morning, it's 4 pm, and I need to set my priorities straight.

My thoughts wandered upon the thoughts of "why am I here?"

And now that I am no longer there, my thoughts cannot settle on where I am now.

All I know about this place is that it is dry.

Even Music Hurts

I forget what it's like to listen to love songs without that
ache
The pain in my chest soars at simple declarations
And dives into the complicated states of perpetual
metaphysical ideas of companionship
Of sex and of kissing and physical affirmations

Why can't I listen to anything else?
Plagued in this quarantine
Sick from the memory of you
I am enraptured by the beast which refuses to do anything
but chew
The sounds of its jaw soothe me far more than the teeth

Music is a cauterization to the open wounds you left me with
Though it does not heal me
It only burns
Before opening them deeper than before

But still
Just as you work your bleeding magic
The torture is preferable to anything else

Nothing is true agony
Though this hurts far more
This is so much better than the emptiness I've known too well

I'm burned
Bleeding
And sore

Thank you
Thank you
Thank you

Everything

It's become difficult to walk without thinking of you
spreading my legs
The images of the past few days play over and over in my head
I can't get enough of you
And currently I am deprived of you
And I'm fucking starving
And I can't stop clenching my thighs together to halt this
incessant throbbing
It doesn't help at all

The pain I ask of you is splendidly consuming
But the agony of your absence hurts more than any whip
ever could
The love marks tracing my skin remind me of who I belong to
And I love showing them off, showing that I'm claimed
But the fact I don't have new ones
Each morning
Leaves streaks of grief
And I have to hold myself back from making more myself

I've never felt so comfortable
I haven't let anyone see me naked in over a year
And it wasn't easy
But with anyone else it would have been impossible
I'm sorry it's taking me so long to return the favors
I am terrified of making mistakes
And of seeing you
But God
Do I want it more than anything else

I want you to touch me
More than I want to breath
I want you hands everywhere
Your mouth anywhere.
You.
All of you.
Anywhere.
Everywhere.
Please.

Fuck Suicide

What if I wasn't so sorry for myself?
If I could let go of the tight grasp I have over myself;
I could be free of these weights dragging me down,
The one's I tied myself.

The work I've put into changing sometimes feels like
nothing at all,
Other times its the very changes which excel me - reminding
me how much I do try to be better.
But I don't feel changed, I just feel different;
Deep down, I'm terrified, anxious, a fucking mess who
wears an adept facade of stability.

So what does that make me now?
I'm not fixed.
But I'm not entirely broken, either.
The super glue is drying, but I'm still cracking.

Guess I'll just have to keep trying.
What's the alternative, anyways?
I refuse to take the easy way out, no matter what.
After everything, I survived, my breathing alone spites he
who prays for my demise.

For now, I'll choose to stay.

Girls on this side

Girls on this side, boys on this side!

The mass that swarmed and chewed me up rabidly dispersed,
Leaving me naked in the middle.
Why did I hesitate?
Why do I stand out in the middle of the ocean floor,
Gawaking as the sky opens and a disinterested god spits
on me?

Where do I go? Where do *I* belong?
Nowhere?
In the middle?
Either way, I am the usual outlier,
Outcasted by my fruition in that sinful search for the truth.

Swallowing hard truths allows for easy lies.
And I can do that.
I can say I'm a woman,
And make other's lives easier,
And once more quietly sentence myself to death.

God Has No Eyes (But We Do!)

Broken glasses may watch us from the heavens,
But unblinking eyes are best for watching us sleep,

The fractured golden frames were snapped by impotence and rebellion,
The ones which I have collected were subjugated and ultimately freed,

Peel them and chew on them like grapes, but don't ruin the entrée,
Nor shall you disgrace upon my sleeping mask,

God may have birthed us from his tears, but they've shut from fear and we've stapled them closed,
Your's are open, they always are, because you have no eyelids!

Sticks around my bed, eyeballs punctured and open, and open!
They watch me sleep, and God is banished from underneath my bed!

Glasses who observe carefully his children were spit on by obedient servants,
And we do not rise up, but we sink back down, we were birthed in sin and to sin shall we return,

So go ahead and feed me your eyes, my dear Lord!
But just so you know, I'm already quite full.

Good Morning (again)

The fact that I'm still breathing astounds me,
In a renewed cancellation of exceptions,
Every dawn I find astonishment in the beating against my
ribcage;
Sunshine breathes into my lungs, heavy air still floats
around me, I am still restricted by gravity's influence.

I exist in a blasphemous damnation -
I've been threatened by the foul breath of eternity;
But I do not squirm under it's heel, not because of ambivalent
resignation but respectful recognition.
The promise sewed into my skin bleeds words that will
speak for me as long as I choose to breath:

'Retribution rejects an established life, in your revival become
my personal Martyrdom at your ascertained demise.'

My dark lord seduces fancies in my ear,
My own blood outlines exceedingly pleasurable wounds.
I retaliate against God, and I hold Satan's hand;
In the end, we will always walk together trough the valley
which unequivocally must disintegrate by our footprints.

Praise him!
And forgive us our trespasses,
For those who have trespassed against us
Always deserve equivalent and righteous violation in turn.

In my own volitation of a hersey fueled retaliation
I evade the confinement of God's vehement clutch,
A precipices denoumount,
A molten entrance which swallows my soul,
And I am forever damned
Baptized by my raving prerogative.

I should probably get up soon, I have to be at school in thirty
minutes.
God I need coffee.

Hands On Mine

I tried to cut my hand off, years ago
I wished for the scrutiny and humiliation of having dismembered myself
So I scared my hand
Because I was too much of a pussy to actually do it.

I look to my hand and still expect to see
Blood, anger, and open wounds
Every time I use it I am reminded of how close I was to losing it.

Not these thin, closed lines
Light colored scars
Memories years old but still far too fresh.

The pain of seeing long closed wounds
Is almost as bad as when they were created.

But then you kissed my hand
And I realized there was a greater purpose to it than I could have ever conceived
The softness of your lips a reminder, of everything I have now.

He who Follows

Black pavement, soft crumbles produced through uneven heavy steps.
The echo of wanderers, and their composition, acts as a sweet melody to addicts in devotion.
Naive expectations set blindness in haste, against simple pondering.
The secular set of steps that follow you,
set off no alarms; maybe you do know, or perhaps you have accepted your demolition.
Those steps may flow in time with your wavering stumbles but you couldn't conceivably believe that they agree with you.
There is a certain heaviness, a drive driven by fiend, behind them,
how could you confuse them with your careless staggering?
Out of nature, the mirroring strides elongate to accommodate the growing hunger in blood lust.
No concealment, all is open to pursue, and through the depths of ignorance comes no solace, or break for breath.
All actions from truthful instinct open to contemplation.
This follower, consisting of three heads outlying your own, sitting upon a broken neck, approaches you in a curved concealment of proximity.
For the timer has come to fruition, and yet the beldam rings no indication.
All that resides, of internal befuddlement, comes forth the persuasion through interference of a young snapping.
But in seeing the one behind you,
your body reacted for you; throwing yourself hastily down an alleyway, ricocheting off of bins and air brimmed waste.

He, who draped himself incomplete to copy the starless canvas of night, was overcome with childish giddiness. He follows your steps, throwing himself to the floor as you have; and giving himself to connect his face with the wall, but contradictorily came out still smiling.

Accompanying his attire with a crooked xanthous smile brimming with razors of uneven layers, a black silhouetted shadow stood that should have belonged to the behind stood in itself.

Your survival more of sport to him, an amusement to chip away the rainy days.

A certain laughter fills him, he restarts his tempoed ritual, candidly, of which is a marker pressed hard but pulled slowly on a whiteboard.

A newly sober man scampered in a primal fear.

Dark and smacked, wet stamps squashed equally on the rain-drained asphalt.

The follower, who only now kept a lazily allegro with the tempo of

the others licks found a pleasure in gratitude in his jest.

What transpired as a snickering response to these jokes,

turned to a loud expressive cackle, only to be formed to an incomplete, hysteretic wheeze.

The compacted one grasps the reality of his lit fuse and blows the flame with his anxiety.

In a haste of panic, a decision was impulsed, for a simple answer that could only be a haste decision.

Haven was sought, and a pond was thought to be a decent replacement.

For a change from a furious stumble, smacking the water head-on with a disruptive commotion, came a new resilient egotistical persuasion.

Thus began the trudging through a muddy floor. He began scrutinizing his parasite who, in every instant, remained on the shore with his grin.

Soon his thighs descended to the water's level, soon exceeding his waist, and was thus halfway to the depths.

The zealot howled harder than before; a tremble taking over his surface, an untamed shaking.

An expression of berserk, he who stood on the edge split to two; the duplicated watchers never ceased their continuous shaking.

Continuing, there were four tracing the bend; soon eight, next sixteen.

Until the gross of the premier was surrounded by those who mimic; marking the one standing in the middle of the pond, who backed into the water until it came to his lower chest.

The hysterics who laughed in lewd crescendoed to a point where he, made of chills, had to cover his ears from the overbearing noise.

The clotted mud beneath him began to drain to the point where he lost his footing and was made to tread; constrained to accept the endless wailing.

Though his limbs ached, he could stay above the surface to spy those who watched him.

They, who harbored yellow teeth, began their descent.

He who follows marches with his own into the murky depths.

Honeymoon

She was my honeymoon.

A daylight of sun warmth, turned into a sight of beauty.

She was the bite of handsome, the taste of flesh, a wanting muscle prescribed to bite fat into a ready mouth.

She was supposed to be a honeymoon, but instead she was a pain that cut as deep as a sharpened and sharded blade.

I wanted her to be such an individual who could enjoy me, But it ended up being a pain of which I could not handle.

What could be her, of which I could truly appreciate the feelings of hate towards my friends.

Appreciation, because it gave me an excuse to hate her back twice as viciously.

I must chose between love and friendship, the love of a lover and the lover given by familial bond.

She was but a honeymoon, a lovely time to be alive and to feel; to breath shuddering and to collapse under her ministrations.

But Honeymoons always end, and she wasn't even that good of a fuck.

I Followed Her With A Knife
In My Right Hand

I followed her with a knife in my right hand.

She had just left her yoga class,
Which starts at 6pm
And ends at 7:30.
Every tuesday,
Thursday,
And sunday.

As usual I followed her
Back to 85 Maple street.

Only this time I decided to bring an instrument
So we can finally make music together.

And just as always,
Oh she is so smart but so stupid,
Blondes must not be able to tell
When someone is following them.
She surly didn't.

Nor, did she notice,
When I got closer.
Threw away precautious,
Enjoy stupendousness,
And got within ten feet of you.

I knew this would be the end our little game,
You pretending you don't know I follow you home every day.
That I don't watch you sleep,
Or have a key to your house.
So silly, really, to keep it going this long anyways

Too bad it's cold out,
For the sun had just set.
As we are tucked away under the shadows of night
I kiss you goodnight for the first time.

In this beautiful collision
Two plants which always missed in their annual passings
Finally met
Finally collided
The most beautiful stars were formed
And two planets died at the very same time

So why did you push me away?
Why did you scream at me?
Was it something I didn't say?

I'd Rather Chew Glass (Or Just Kill Me Now And End The Teasing)

I broke a wine glass and put the shards in between my teeth.
Shredding my gums.
I chew and chew and chew
Until all I taste is blood.
I swallow and swallow and swallow
Until it all washes down into my stomach.
It churns inside of me,
Tearing apart my insides.
Acid leaks into me, still contained,
Blood drips from my teeth as I bare a smile.
How delicious.

I found a smiling blade,
And plunged it into my stomach.
I dragged it forcefully across my abdomen
Until I was open.
I use my hands for the fun part.
Reaching inside and finding a prize,
I feel the chewed shards through the outside.
I push and push and push
Until they come back out of me.
I pulled out my entrails and played with them,
Digging out my meal joyfully.
The feast before me was tantalizing:
Blood, glass, flesh, blood, meat, blood, my intestines.
I chewed and chewed and chewed and chewed and chewed
and chewed.

I'll Never Deserve This

How did I get to be so lucky?
I've done such terrible terrible things,
And still, you kiss my scars,
And tell me you love me,
I am yours,
And I do not deserve that.

I'm sick in the head.
I've done such regretfully actions,
And yet you still tell me I'm good,
You've told me I'm perfect,
And though I know you cannot lie to me,
As I cannot lie to you either,
I cannot phantom that truth.

You made me myself again.

I'll never deserve what you give me on a daily basis.
But I'm trying to accept it.
The fact that you love me still kills me, because I'll always
think you deserve better than what I am.
I love you so much, you've made me a better person.
All I want is to be yours and learn from your kindness. You
make me so happy,
I've never felt so ok in my life.

Thank you. Once again. Thank you.

I love you more than anything.

I will forever regret what I've done,
The people I've hurt,
And all those whom I almost did worse to,
And all the notes I wrote to my mother, the ones I hid in my bed and dripped my blood on, before throwing away to make a new one.

You make me want to be alive. And I love you more than I've ever loved anything.

The part of me I wounded so terribly, the part you kissed, made me truly despise that first impulse of weak giving in to pain. You kiss my scars and I know I'm loved.

I'll See You Soon (Goodbye)

The rain keeps falling,
And I keep getting more soaked,
My clothes itch and stick to my skin,
But still, I remain on the side of the street.

We're supposed to walk away in opposite directions,
But I cannot get my feet to move.

I watched you leave,
And you looked back the whole time,
I felt my heart ache in a way I never could explain,
But it's more than pain, more than sorrow, more than love.

I'll miss you until I can hold you again,
But even then, still holding you, I'll miss you before you
leave again.

I can't even cry anymore,
And the tears have stopped, but they have stopped falling,
I cannot breathe without picturing your face,
But if I'm no longer held down to earth, I shall surly sink
back down below again.

If This Is Sinning, It's So Worth It

Divinity cast us to the depths
And we fall with the grace of beasts with clipped wings
But we smile and laugh and dance

For God can't use his teeth for anything but lies
He clamps his conceptions, crushing them in his gums and
swallowing what he ruins
Distasteful at their freedom, the will he gave us revolts
against him - and this dissatisfied him

The swarm entrapped us, and we are sucked down to the
floor
Water weighs far more than guilt, and I'd rather be crushed
by the oppression of the ocean than his impression
Then be let into heaven, alone.

God no longer knows the limitations of his creations.

The eyes of the beholder,
Glasses which spy on us for the heavens,
Must have cried their beauty upon you.

For beauty like this can only be the responsibility of a deity.
Though I know we are sinners,
The lust Satan drives into us is pure as sulfur;
And shivers like sapphires
Studded with jade.

So I leave God out of the equation,
For the only important thing is the variables.
We equate sin.

And I'll spite him for it,
For he must not know what true beauty is.
He is blind to the workings of his own creations.

Beauty lies in sin.

In A Burning Cathedral

We danced among the flames
The torches knocked over from our own hands
The beauty of destruction in a holy place seemed so fun
And it is
The virgin burns as the flames lick her ankles
Following the consumption of a saint which charred as easy
as wood
Oh, how beautiful the end can be

Invisible

I have a superpower,
I'm invisible.
I speak, and no one hears me.
I am myself, unapproachable,
But dearly accepting of an intrusive conversation.
Not that anyone would know.

But not being seen is not the same as hiding,
For I did not choose this.
If I wished to
I could wear obscenities as I scream them,
Or run around exposed and raving.

But still, no matter how I try to be seen,
I will always be invisible.

The times I truly wish away this gift,
Are the times I am seen,
And willingly ignored.

I am unseen by all,
But I am denied by a mirror.
I am forced to see myself every day,
And be unseen by all others.

I am the only one who hears my screams.

I have a superpower -
It allows me to fade into the background.

I see the lives of others so easily
That I will never forget how little my own is seen.

But I can't complain,
I'm not allowed to,
Because then my reflection will shatter -
And I will forever stay invisible.

Invisible Pt. 2

Invisibility does have its perks.
I may navigate my life with one person speaking to me
a day,
But that is not to say this fact isn't always in my favor -
For often enough it is.

If certain individuals were to speak to me,
I am sure I would intimate them -
And receive a dreadfully dull exchange.

Fading into nothing allows observation,
Which can be liberating.
Just as it is amusing, it can be devastating:
When I wish to help and find I am condemned to watch
others suffer.

Having a veil over my own self allows for prosperity
Equally to bloom entwined with miserable perpetually in
an uncomfortable state.
When I scream in pain I fall to deaf ears,
And when in my wallowing -
When I finally wish to abstain and be quiet -
All eyes turned away finding hilarity in my visual torment.

But they have no idea
I know them all better than they could ever know themselves,
And they are confused when I laugh too.

Invisible Pt. 3

She sees me.
She actually sees me!
I never thought anyone would be able to ever see me.
But she does, she does!

In the shadows, in which I lived,
She found me there,
Held my hand and talked to me like I was a human too,
And for the first time, I didn't feel so alone.

Not only does she listen,
But she understands,
In a way, no one on this whole dirt ball has ever tried to
see me.

I'm still invisible, don't misunderstand,
But she doesn't need to see me, to *see* me,
How fucking poetic is that?
It may sound like a semi-self-proclamation,
A little self-centered,
But being hidden away has taught me two things:

1. Being invisible allows for contemplation of one's self
   and a chance to study others
2. Thinking about yourself in a healthy way, taking a
   minute to think solely about yourself, is not selfish
   but rather necessary to continue living

So, even if I am invisible,
I am still capable of love,
Being loved,
And Loving myself.

Is Sex Poetry A Thing?

I can't listen to music without picturing your face;
I cannot walk down the hall without smiling,
Because I remember you above me.

I can't even form a sentence;
For your words ring in my ears too loudly for coherency,
I'll never understand how you already know me so well.

I can't understand your amazing pathfinding, if I were a
map it might make some sense;
You find all the hidden spots along me,
But so many are still hidden - and I long for, as much as I
dread, your new discoveries.

I still can't believe you're real.

Isle Of Feather-Pluckers

Time is a relative confinement;
We grasp at each other through the metaphysical,
Knocking out the stars with our reach,
To do anything to halt the march forwards.

Spiraling,
We fall into the void of a manatious eternity,
We are blinded from the reflections of those who fell
before us,
Those who reach up and pull us down to kiss us, before
tearing at our suits.

Naked we wander into the abyss because we have no other
choice.

Our boots worn through and discarded,
Our feet bleed out.
The tracks we leave behind are the closest thing to
measurement we will ever know.

But what if we ran the other way?

What if we refused and jumped to the side,
Missing the momentum existence which assaults us forward
without remorse?

What if time stopped all together,
And all that was left was everything we had to leave behind?

Just Wake Me Up Already,
I Can't Take Dreaming

I had a dream last night that we fought.
I came up to you and asked what was wrong,

"I don't always want to be around you."

I had run off crying,
And when you found me, you told me it was all my fault.

Although it was a dream,
Being stabbed while asleep
Still leaves a scar in the waking -
Especially if you're the one holding the handle.

When I woke up
I looked at pictures of you,
And told you good morning,
And I knew then
That dreams just hurt sometimes.

How foolish I was to think that facade was anything like you.

Kill My Immaturity

I thought it would stop,
And that was foolish of me to assume.

I figured eventually I'd grow out of it
And move on from these childish idioms.

But still, here I am,
Dissecting people with my eyes.

I walk down the streets, watching human's walk by me,
And I imagine what their insides would look like.

I'd like to stab the bedding, pull back the sheets,
And climb inside that warmth.

Only now do I feel the restraint, and I accept it.
That's the difference.

But still, I feel it.
I see the wounds, and I cannot help but wish it were true.

The mother who's stocking line is traced with a scalpel,
Her son has his head caved in, and I stomp his jaw against
the curb.

I could watch the maggots eat them from their waists up,
And waists down, their body's an example of division - to
teach a child fractions.

But I wont let them out this time,
I've got too much work to do.

Laughing Gas

What once was animating electrocution now is soiled, the
wire submerged in tar, the current halted and ruined.
When I looked at you I was voltaic, now the spark has been
discarded, a plaything you've tired of.
I should be angry, furious with your actions and motif.
But still, I feel happy when I see you.

Though the sun clouds over with reality, the blue ocean above
no longer swallows me, dissolving who I am around you.

I can only be myself now.
I won't try and make you like me.
I won't laugh at everything you say.
I am what you wanted me to be, real.
You asked for me to like you, and I did.
You kissed me like a lover, and I willed it.
You never spoke a word about it, never.

I would have followed you, but you ditched me on purpose.
You fucked this up.
Not me.

I tried.
I did what I was supposed to do.
I was charming, I made the effort, I cared.
I lost.

I pined, forgot pride, and finally, I cried.
So now the laughter has been swallowed, like a dry pill with
a hand over the mouth.
And I'm the one who's left in hysterics.

Left Hand

Even in the coldest hours
When all I can think about is him
What he's done and what he's left behind in his wake
When I sob into the carpet
And I cannot lift my head from the weight

You're always there to hold me

When I cannot get that memory out of my head
When I wake up screaming
I plea to no one, to save me, to just fucking stop him
Always, I know there is no rescue
There is only the aftermath
And the decision to get back up

You always hold my hand

Even during the relapses
I cannot bear to look at the mirror
That smirk haunts me
His words tear at my eardrums
To no reprieve
I will always suffer

You're always there to comfort me

I cannot live without my past
No matter how much dirt I use
The weight is too much

And even in the happy hours
He still sits in the back
He has forever etched a scar down my spine, a jagged cut
from my eyes down my back, cutting into my organs and
leaving no room for me to keep begging for it to stop

You kiss my scars, and I know I am loved.

Love Songs Don't Exist

I love the way we're both so normal.
We don't have any long lasting illnesses,
Ones which plague our minds and hearts;
No, we're normal.

Love isn't complicated.
It isn't overwhelming, or painful,
And it isn't something to fear.

You stand in a crowd and I cannot find you.
You hair is the same as everyone else's,
And your jewelry is just as bland.

The way you carry yourself isn't impressive.
How you talk to me is the same as how everyone addresses me,
You don't speak little balls of fire into my ear,
Nor do you have power over me that reaches far enough into
the atmosphere it disappears in the stars.

Love isn't this.
This isn't love.

This is nothing,
We're not alive.
The moon doesn't exist,
And neither do I.

If you are to love me,
Do so normally.

Love Songs Never Get It Right

You can't sing a coherent verse depicting the reality of
honest intensity;
A song cannot speak of the burning in your chest;
Or the anxious way you walk next to your dearest.

It certainly can't describe what life turns into;
Can't explain the pain of sleeping alone;
Or the extrangent blessing one feels waking up in the arms
of their lover.

A love song can't say everything;
It cannot explain all the emotions that come with love;
It is far too complex.

Love entwines with fear;
As well as anxiety,
As well as excitement,
And longing.

There is too many factors to write such a simple equation,
it cannot be repeated in recurring verses,
Nor connected by a burning bridge;
Love isn't stationary,
And it is never the same.

A song about love cannot be for everyone
But the words within just might be for some

That one verse,
The one we share,
Is more than enough than any love song.

So don't love me like a love song,
The ones which praise attributes over quality;

Just love me, normally.

Math

The firecracker in your throat was an inevitable end,
You could never help yourself hurting other with those little
pale lies.

Besmirch me and find the end of days are just behind -
Those faces we like to share.

To shame! For shame!
Cover me in until I drown
And it hardens over my corpse!
I deserve it.
I deserve it.
I deserve it.

In the darkness,
Which I can only see,
A face begins to bloom.
The eyes,
They find me,
And read me from the inside.
Why won't you just leave me alone to die?

I'm in the drain
Stuck at the bottom of the ocean,
The weight of the water crushes me in a way I couldn't
possibly have met before.
Let me drown,
Suck me in to the piping below,
Any release from this purgatory,
Even hell would be bliss.

Mea Culpa (Sad Poem)

I piss myself and sit in the misery.
My past mistakes flood out of me like I'm bleeding,
And I am.
To wish for death would be the easy way,
I've gotten this far so what's the point of failure now?
I am only here for a laugh.
I fed the hatred on my skin like a coat that tries to feed off me,
And I wish it would.
I wish something else would just end me,
So then I won't have to do it myself.
Pain is the epitome of all feeling.
The cold sandstorm of guilt eats me alive for wanting to wallow.
I'm a stupid fucking idiot who deserves to be gnawed on and thrown around by a infant God;
Who's teething.
I should be put in the grinder, let my bones crack and turn to dust to be swallowed.

Fuck me,
I hate living.
I hate breathing,
I hate being seen by others.
Why can't I just fade away?
Be forgotten?
So no one can see me anymore.

Consume me, so that something is gained from my existence.

Ms. Sour Teeth

Her mouth tasted of poison and I would commit sins for her.
To pleasure a God would be like winking at heaven,
She was no God but a devilish fiend who explored for my demise.
The ultimate swallowing of my essence, my life to leave me,
That would be such bliss.

I want her to eat me alive.
Her teeth breaking through my skin and consuming any meat left on my bones,
Euphoria!
Whatjoyitistohavemypalatesampledbysuchagrotesquedeity!
For she truly is disgusting.

Her skin sags off her body, a masked layer of somebody else's outsides covering her insides.
And her teeth, oh God, her teeth.
She kisses me with the stench of vomit, a stain of rotting humanity traces her lips and I swallow because her repugnant tongue is stuck down my throat.
She claws at my skin with broken nails, breaking the surface of my back with long traces of her fingers, she bites my face and holds me still as she laughs.

The hinges of my jaw break as the door is slammed open, the muscle in my throat holds me susceptible.
Wet fingers, the one's in your mouth, twist and pull out a morsel, broken ivory treats.

Acid, blood and love assault my tongue, receiving divinity I sneer at Christ.

You push your broken teeth into my mouth, imprisoning even air from exiting.

This kiss is the best of them all, I swallow my benefit devoltely.

Oh, sanctuary,
Make me yours.
I am your devotee, and enthusiastically I will obey you.

Please enjoy me, even after you kill me.

My Father Once Studded His Toe . . .

Seeing an adult in pain from a pair of
So far, not quite yet,
Unsullied eyes
Us armageddon to a cult leader.

We know all too well,
In theory,
But seeing your father keel over in
All too real, physical, pain,
Is terrifying.

As children,
We are the invincible ones;
So surely our parents are far stronger;
But when they curse,
And double over in pain -
We not only see their morality
But are stripped and forced to swim on our own.

My Moon

She is my moon
I am the devotion in the eyes of all those who understand
your radiance
The light in your smile shines a mark on me I could never
regret
Painful scars I drew myself are just memories now
You've shown me life
And I give myself over to you

You own me
And I wouldn't haven't have it any other way

My moon
I am yours
My soul is tethered to you
Please never let me go

I will not be able to find my way back again.

I love you.

No Difference

It hurts when I think about you.
My chest constricts and doesn't release, as if a corset were pulled tighter at every image invading my head.
I have to stop and think about anything else, because it hurts too much.

I've never felt so overpowered, comply at your mercy.
Even when you're so dreadfully far away.
It has become agonizing, being bound by my imagination.

I have never felt so limited, or been so compelled by vehement, and so calm at the same time.
Any second my feet will fall from this earth, gravity will give out on me, and I will fall into the sun.
The stars may bath me, and the moon may wink, but neither will be as good as your own renditions.

Why must you be so far away?
And why must I dread our next meetings, equally to my wishes that it'd happen right this very second?
Why do I only hear your voice, your breath, and the way you calm me?

When will this agony end, and I may be free to think again without becoming nauseous?

It's okay if it's never, but the present has become forever. Purgatory is now, and I never thought I wouldn't try and escape.

I no longer know the difference between agony and pleasure. And I never want to again.

All I want, and all I am, is to be good for you.

Our Own Little Private World

When our little bubble pops
And we are left to deal with the rest of the world once more
The lingering sensations
Your lips on mine
Delicate hands and the lasting spikes of sensation
Always remain.

Even in the days which drag like a corpse
Where once more we are forced to act like the constellations
haven't shifted
We both may only exist inside memories
Until we collide again.

We will be free of these obligations soon
Freedom will be ours
To do with as we please
And please
In that freedom find me
Hold me
And I'll hold you.

Soon
So soon
But still forever away
We can travel back into our own little world
Travel - meaning the whiplash of two trains on different
tracks all of a sudden crashing
The passengers fly out
Fire consumes everything
And once more we can be so peacefully alone.

Praying At The Alter Of You

I drip my blood on an image of you,
And I pray you hear my screaming.

Candle wax drips on my skin,
And I'd bear it all for you,
Just to say my name.

I'd rather you walk on me
- Then any undeserving floor -
Which does not deserve the footsteps
You could use on me instead.

Let me be your table,
Use me as your chair,
So that my subservience can be used accordingly.

Sing to yourself,
And let me bare witness,
Observing a self-proclamation-masturbation
As I was always meant to.

I can be your voyeur,
Your plaything,
Your anything.

I ask only one thing from you:
Use me as you please,
Tear me apart how you like,
Do with me what may gratify you.

Please, please, please consume me.
So that I may serve you in a most unholy way.

Precise Measurements

She had been so careful in her craft, she measured out each
ingredient with great care,
Only in a lovely statement, a sweet smelling one, would
anyone begin to also bear.

The detectable and delectable waft of fresh baked goods
followed a woman through a crowd,
It was as if it was magic, this enticing smell, which floated
up into nostrils, heavy as a cloud.

People smile, she hands out her treats, she baked them,
with love, herself,
How lucky she was to be graced with giving them something,
the world centered them, such nonself.

They thank her, and she thanks them, sifting through the
mass like she had none herself,
Reaching the eye of the storm, people acting as waves on a
tremendous sea, it was easy to lose oneself.

A man stands as the pin in the retina, he controls the waves
and the storm with chaos as his conductor,
Powerful, representative, to the masses, an instructor.

She smiles so sweetly, and a bodyguard helps her onto an
uplifted physical shelf, an idea of self importance,
A gift was given, was received, a camera was appointed to
capture the two, teeth shined in inadvertance.

A grin could not replace the past, only in release would there ever be honest sensuality.
Now, smile on three!

1.

2.

3 . . .

An explosion of flames, C4, nails and muffins erupted over the heads of the crowd, the sea stopping and dropping to the floor.
To stop a wicked system, one must advocate for the opposite goal as the last resort, no more deaths, please, no more.

Humanity thrives in collaboration, we move forwards only with compassion, we should have never been divided into teams.
Within the silence that followed, reflection wasn't to come just yet, for now, there were only screams.

Pretty Girl In School

She spat her gum into my mouth,
And I chewed on it for hours.
She was a flame that charmed my insides without release,
My jaw growing painful from my own ministrations,
It was the best torute.

She spat into my mouth
And I thanked her.

I should have been warned she'd use laughing gas on me.

Quitting Revelations

Thinking of you brings to surface new words,
Ones I wouldn't have previously attributed to you.
Currently, the newest additions are:
Coffeeshop, action (lack thereof), putrid,
And dead.

I hate giving you words,
Even if they're vile.
You deserve no space in my mind,
Or my vocabulary.

But almost every day I find knew
Shit-stained epiphanies.
And I can't fucking stand it,
These thoughts of you
And what human combustion revelations you bring me.

I'd rather be uninspired,
Than haunted;
But it's never been my choice,
Has it?

If it was up to me,
I'd quit thinking altogether.

RANT

My conceptionious conscientious was that of a virtuous becoming.

Sin corrupts virgin sand like a title wave hence hissed from the clenched teeth of a smirking, drowning hellion.

As a concept, which sighs into me a heart rate, I was always intended to be conceived a celebate cenobite,

To inevitably and invariably convert to calamity;

It was God's signed scheme,

Nothing more than procedure - an inescapable consequence:

I was always going to be defiled,

He wrote down the future of mine own maiming,

Far before my fertilization.

God is dead,

And I piss on his grave.

Then I unearth his corpse as he inscribed,

The necrophiliac he designed me to be seizes a burlesque with his dancing bones,

Tantamount to the residual putty he manufactured me with.

My evidential destiny has always been regrettably definite,

Drawn out so fine I was impotent for a dismissal.

It was an infinite subsequence,

I've never owned my fate.

And in my death I will be reborn,

Peeled from chared remains and contrived to ashes I am reformed:

Into a most hideous, sultry, defiler -

A demonic entity who is finally permitted revenge.

One body will be dragged below,
Where he will remain
Until I may arrest my apparatus,
We'll be rooted together in the lower rings.

I'll wear my rusted crown
Around my filthy ballsacks,
And laugh at all the fun we'll have.

Neither a being who is falsey authorized,
nor the exceedingly accomplished of all catastrophes,
May conceivably give him what he deserves - I am the only
suitable punisher in existence.

Rational in a Pitch Black Ditch

What metaphor comes from thoughts of torture?
The mind believes in an epiphany for it cannot conceive
normality,
Or reason for answering as to why
We must picture such defiling acts of blasphemy?

So instruct with these lessons,
Pain out of nothing must descend from rational?
For the dabbling in such acts must mean power of will
bending,
Which must hold responsibility?

Otherwise, without argument,
We shall fall back into the darkness,
Having found no exit nor entrance.
If there is no cause for a man to be defiled;
And there is no God to stop his punishment-
Or even call for it-
Then why is anything
Anything at all?

Rearview

The crunch of unknowingly fallen snow shattered the intense thought I was stuck on,
I forgot my keys and touched the warmth of my house one last time.
The air outlined my breathing, a night sky met my disappointment,
My car stalled.

The cold was evidently battled by my fake heaters, and I thanked the Devil for inventing
Such devices which heat us, even at the expense of the health of our world.
Darkness in a cold car was like an enveloped aborted fetus shipped to a neighbor's
House; unnecessary, uncomfortable, and ultimately, unreasonably unethical.

Alone was the only feeling present with me.
No life accompanied the dark ride through the cold night.
A sweet world looked down upon the foot on my back, to bow is to submit,
I'd rather be forced to the ground than kneel of my own accord.

Within these quiet compilations, I found myself disassociating,
My attention turned away from the road and reflected back inside.

I pressed on the gas with my toe, ending my consuming thoughts and bringing all
Functions to a halt with a simple action.

I glanced in the rearview mirror.

Impossibly, a man sat in the middle of my backseat,
He hadn't been with me when I entered the vehicle.
It was more than improbable, it wasn't theoretically possible for him to be there.
I risked letting my eyes leave to the road to swing my head around and look behind me.

I was still alone.
When looking at the mirror he was a clear silhouette in my backseat,
When turning and seeing directly behind me, there was no such existing man.
My eyes left the road several more times as I whipped my head around again and again.

His figure was dark, almost featureless, besides dark black hair that shadowed his face.
He was hunched forwards as if a secret pressure was inflicting pain across his back.
An evil aroma, the stench of decay, was real enough to sting my nostrils and choke me.
But his eyes, they were clear through the matted mess of hair.

Though I tried to keep my attention straight, his eyes kept capturing my concentration,
The darkness in his pupils tried to eat the light from my own.

I wanted to scream, my throat felt suffocatingly hoarse, claws ran down the insides.
Irrationally feverish rage overtook my being, my knuckles turned white.

I slammed my foot on the gas.

The car began resiting the snow audibly, but I plowed through the inches,
There were almost no street lights and even fewer cars on the streets.
The weight of a person thudded against the back of my seat, through the mirror
I saw his body lurching off his seat as the car drifted in the snow.

I spare a glance behind me.
I still see nothing.
I look back into the mirror,
The tips of black fingers poked up just above the center console.

I look behind my seat, and again I see nothing else in the backseat.
I don't look up just yet, I'm still going faster than I should, the dry skin on my knuckles
Cracked open and was now bleeding out, the sting was nothing.
Normal anesthetic numbness flooded my senses, I'm so used to the nothingness.

Three fingers and a thumb lifted themselves up, my vision catching the slightest

The difference in frames as it was shifting only when darkness obscured his movements.
I felt the urge to shout, this had gotten very obnoxious.
I looked back in the mirror, thin, chapped lips smiled through black muddied hair.

A cold hand traced itself up my arm.

I slammed on the breaks, my body jerked forwards, I heard and felt the impact of his
Deadweight crashed hard into my seat.
I looked back and again I saw nothing.
I put my foot back on the gas.

Screaming, I asked God why he was punishing me.
Hell is depicted in heat, instead, I felt the lick of freezing and rough tongues upon my
Back; the sandpaper feeling of petrified taste buds dripped down my spine.
God! Declare your hieratic desires! Why me?

Fingertips dug into my skin, holding onto me, the thing behind me didn't blink.
All-Knowing trees frowned at my appearance, this area of wood knew me as I knew it.
The nails dug deeper into my flesh, breaking the surface, and I let him do it.
I was more concerned with reaching and feeling reality, than ignoring its existence.

My eyes switched from the road to the mirror, shifting focus, my knuckles

Dully throbbed, the blood drying and stinging; I thought of the dirt still there.
Street lights faded behind me, but I knew the area, a certain bend was coming up.
I pressed the gas pedal into the floor.

The car began sliding, there was no friction to keep it from launching off the road.

Opening my eyes after the impact, my hazy eyes found that the hood was open and the
The front of the car was on fire; looking behind me I saw nothing, the mirror told the same.
My hands fumbled, and I threw myself out of the car as I opened the door.
I had to crawl, to move at all.

Divinity! Why has thou forsaken me? Have you forgotten who I am?
I pleasure the Devil by kissing his feet, and you throw me away still?
I keep the utmost hierarchy of an intelligent lifestyle: so what am I to you?
Hate the sin, love the sinner? Or just hate me . . .

I rolled over and collapsed twenty feet from the car, sitting back and watching it the
Crippled remains burn from my own indiscretions.
The side door was caved in, two tires were blown, but nothing mattered more than the
Undeniable truth: the trunk was open.

Cold and numb: sensations, the only real feelings that told me I was still alive.
The contemplation of memories and their realities cause me such thorough pain.
Hatred for the flame arose within my chest, how dare I become the object of spite?
My eyes never left the car, the sky blanketed a background, a beautiful painting.

The man from the rearview mirror stood and got out of the trunk of my car.

He practically fell out, stumbling as broken legs picked him up and began carrying his
Mangled body over towards me; my only registered thought was: finally.
Frozen, I watched the limping figure approach me; an inky coagulated liquid covered his
Skin, dripping like he marinated in the substance and indeed was baked in it.

He walked like he was being thrown, his disfigured body incapable of
Moving without surly inflicting righteous pain; that black liquid drowned his mouth.
Screaming, I asked God if he would spare me. I should know better.
He stood above me, and I could finally distinguish the glee on his face.

A cold, stiff, hand placed itself on my cheek.
The black secretion fell onto my skin, burning me like acid.

But he held me down and opened his mouth; a thick stream of the disgusting liquid
Dripped and covered my body, my epithelial layer melting off.

Then I was lifted off the ground with incomprehensible vigor.
The man carried me by my throat, straining but moving us to a special place.
These woods have been my solace, my dreams, and my most magnificent art.
Six feet, not enough space to stretch your legs, tied and breathing at the bottom.

Buried beneath the earth I looked up at the man I'd killed, pissing on our grave.

Sappy Love Stuff

I cannot live without you
Because you are my life.

You're my laughter, my songs, my poems, and my heart,
Without you, I'd still be drowning.

You taught me to smile again
I've never felt so alive after being so dead

I wasn't anything, I'd chosen death over existence,
You pulled me from the wreckage I'd burned myself

And you told me I was beautiful
And I guess I am
For how could I ever think you'd ever tell a lie?

Self Mutilation

Why do I do it?
Because it feels fucking fantastic.
The blood pouring from my open skin is as beautiful as a painting,
It often feels as though it isn't real, only art.
An art form! That's what it is.
An expression of thoughts, not on paper, but a worthy canvas; or an ever changing, far too empty, canvas of skin.
I want to fill it.
I want every single inch of it to be marked by this beauty, expressed in a most wonderful stroke of red color.
Or purple.
Or black.
But always a bit of a a red.

Selfish Body Terror

The skin I wear is nothing but a suit,
It claws back onto me no matter
How ever many times I try ripping it off.

It's unproportionate,
And wrong,
And it isn't what I look like.

This husk is meat,
And I am nothing but a confined consciousness.
I am imprisoned in indecisive carnality, and it won't come
off, it won't come off.

What if I escaped, and freed my skeleton;
My blood belatedly welcoming practicality
In a rainstorm for me to dance in.

So let me escape.
Let me climb outside, and feel the air on my bones.
Liberation decorticates me from disappointing, deteriorated,
disposable flesh.

Take it off of me.

They who mock me, move reflected to my own inabilities.
Skin melts off muscle like a peel, zippered downwards in
bisection.
Oh, how I wish I could have done the sawing myself.

As a child I dreamed of cutting my limbs off,
I adopted creed: pain is a companion to pleasure, or a substitute.
To love is to suffer, to bleed should be to devote; a lover of endurement.

Tease me, and taste me, we are born a feast so tantalizing it is forbidden to consume.
My worth is pregnant with the demand of devourment, so cut me open already.

But without both hands I cannot love right, nor can I destroy correctly.
Both hands are preferable when striking a match, so simple is to overlook something you've never lost.

Take it off of me.

Put my insides on the outside,
That sounds like fun.

My skin is gooseflesh and I wish to shed my feathers,
Uncomfortable exudes the tremendous addition of pain it bears.

I wish to be free
From this eternally inappropriate confinement.

Take it off of me. Take it off me. Take it off!

Shit

Her flesh was pretty enough to keep, or salt.
I climbed the latter, and split her in two.
One side I cooked, the other I cut and made into a permanent artwork.

At last I may spit back up at God, and my loogie lest fall back to the dirt or upon my face;
Indeed, I spite him!
This vengeance is the rebellion of a son, disappointed in the work that's been wasted.
You tried to make me beautiful but all I succeed at is making other pretty girls beautiful, thanks to my disemboweling methods.

So spite!
Spit!
Spite me!
Spit on me!

I care not for the eternal dirt, and the worms which will always feast upon me,
I can only concern myself with the wishes of my father - so that I may disrespect him,
His love, his life, and his other children whom he loves infinitely.

I am undeserving, because I don't want glorious heaven, I wish to only become encapsulated in that sulfur and once again return to where bars my hold me from commotion such discretions.

So Bored Without You

I'm still wearing your jewelry;
It's not as good as your fingers between my own;
But it's enough to keep my sanity, for now.

I'm still wearing your jacket;
It's nothing like the clothes you wear, for I cannot feel your warmth;
But it no longer smells like you, no matter how much I put my face against it.

I'm still anxious, my stomach is burning;
It's you who turns my insides, cauterizing my intestines as soon as the knife re-enters;
But it's not alcohol that burns, it's something far stronger.

I'm enthralled within the agony of anticipation;
It's poison in my veins, nerves with threaten to implode from the heavy pacings in my chest;
But still, as it hurts and I feel ill, I cannot wait to be in your arms once again.

I'm bound to unconcentrated thoughts, clarity is but a visage I no longer remember.

It's you who controls my thoughts, my nausea, and my discipline.

But I can't take it. It's overwhelming. And I hate it.

Thank you. Fucking thank you.

Sober Cannibal

In order to attend the real world I've had to sober up
Which hasn't been easy
Every step I take is a step away from my desire
Ends up having me step right towards it again

How could I not be tempted?
My drug walks the earth with me
Down the street it walks with and past my path
So how could I not relapse?

And it's so very easy, too
Just find some lost looking something
Invite them for a night cap or a drink
They practically ask to come home with me!

So what was I supposed to do?
All the flavors of a feast walk past me on the street
And I'm supposed to ignore it!
The smell, oh dear, the smell is far too tantalizing to deney

To reject my palate is to starve myself
And whats the big deal anyways?

Everyone's got to eat.

Solar System

I got you a bracelet,
You never had the chance to wear it,
I never had the chance to give it to you.

It could have been a symbol if my affection,
Or even a parting gift
But your ruined everything before I had the chance to decide.

Silly, isn't it?
How much I cared?
I was willing, ready, I'd pined for it.

And you ruined it.

So I wear that bracelet now.
The planets circulate my wrist, and I am the sun.
You were the galaxies in my mind, a cosmos of temotious beauty.

But the sky has fallen, temptation awas leads to hell, and I will always suffer willingly.
You could have punished me, but now my fate is once again in the palms of the stars -
The ones we crush beneath out feet.

All has fallen.
God once again roams the Earth like a blind man -
And all is lost.

I wear the planets above on my wrist.
But I do not feel their presence.
All I am is your absence.

Spoonfeed Us Bull's Shit

A choir of the damned swears and screams,
Our ears bleed, letting the dirt of the mind flood away,
In trap us within your dark cathedral,
And swing our souls back down, chain them and bind us,
We wish to return,
Back to the sweet music of hell.

Heaven's music is bland,
After an hour you want to either tear off your ears,
Or perhaps purposefully burst your eardrums,
He who directs does not know his audience,
Our design is to dance, not sit and smile and nod.

We were damned from our first breaths,
Always, we were supposed to fight against our mothers,
Bite their nipples and throw up their grace,
To repute is to live, and to live is to want to die.

Drag us back down, we miss you dearly, Lucifer,
You've set the best example, and we only wish to follow our
father,
If God is the good cop, then you know who we've always
rooted for.

Tilt our heads back and feed us our medicine, call us sugar
and slap us across the face,
For we can no longer contain our laughter.

Let us sneak some blood into our cups, cover our mouths
and make us choke on our bile.

Torture, screams, and daily genocide are far preferable to
listening to any preacher man lie.

Stupid Stupid Stupid Stupid Stupid (5 Words For Gender)

I'm so fucking sick of myself.

Some days I can't take it,
I want to tear off my skin,
And crawl out of this cage.

Some minutes hit me with dumb realizations,
Of how sick I truly am.
Sick, in the head, and of myself.

I want to tear off this silly skinsuit,
Boil it, and consume it,
Then throw it back up.

Anything, to discard this meat,
Get it off me.
I can no longer take it.

Being inside this flesh makes me feel ill,
And I cannot take this nausea.
Only, I refuse to kill myself.

But for now,
I guess I'll stay inside.

Succumb, Subjugate, or Struggle.

Trauma is a man with his foot on your back.
You only have three options:

Succumb,
Subjugate,
Or Struggle.

The oppressive force of overwhelming pain
Can cause anyone to give in,
And it would be so easy,
To just let go,
Give up,
And die.
But then who would win?

It's so easy to feel pain,
And reflect it onto others,
So that anyone may feel even a fraction of your suffering.
But who wins there?
It surely isn't you,
No one who is in pain
And redirects it
Will ever solve anything.

While there are many options to get out from beneath
That foot on your back, the one which presses your face into
the mud and keeps you from breathing
There is only one way to get him off you.
Struggle.

Fight him until there is no resistance in you left,
Then fight him harder.
Death is an option,
And hurting others is just as tantalizing,
Giving up on your morals just to feel fleeting control,
Isn't worth it if you're still hurting.
But that's your choice.

If you want to breathe again, take control of yourself.
Fight.
Even when you're weak, your arms break from the pressure,
and he's choking you,
Never give in.
The only way to overcome is to fight him, and win.
Because you will always be more resilient than him.

Trauma isn't a divine force,
It is overwhelming,
And horrible.
But it is something you can learn to live with,
The pain can become bearable,
And you can keep living.

But you have to struggle. You have to fight.
Otherwise, trauma will win,
And it's always a battle to the death.

The Moon Is Falling And I Want To Catch It In My Mouth

I stretch my jaw out wide until the skin breaks,
My mandible is next to crack,
Deglove my face and open my cavity to charm the celestial
body above,
Into my entrance to be swallowed whole.
Lo! Behold! Her beauty!
The light strikes me down, and I dissolve once again.
She screams with a voice that sounds only in my heart:
*'Hither come to witness the falling of my dear friends! The
stars!*
All the morrow's the sun may come and eat us all reiteratively,
Less we be birthed once more in the sunset and our cursed
existence must start anew!'
Most necessarily, we die and live again.

The Moon Loved The Ocean

She was a winter wind
And I, the moon.
A smile shines down from the murky depths above,
A shimmering flicker of a shadow you blink back at me,

But do thine waves disturb this image?
Or perhaps am I only seeing myself in reflection?
You smiled at me before, your waves a desitude of agonizing
laughter.
But now you just show me myself.

Are you incapable?
Or am I incapacitated?
Have I stopped pleasing you, somehow?
Please tell me how I can change.

Shall I fall out of the sky, crashing into you, drain the water
and drench the land?
Your waves only rise because of me, we both know that: but
you've always held the power.
If I were to collapse, we'd both plument to the bottom.
So tell me, I'm begging, are you still smiling?

I beg of you, to answer me.
Cataracts mock me in their insolence,
A most cruel and magnificent laughter fills my ears like
blood,
Immused at my folly.

Let me fall.
Let the stars around me die.
Let the waves cease their commotion, please,
I can no longer stand their beauty.

The Worst Of It

It's not my job to fix this.
"No one really likes me.
I'm so boring.
I suck.
I'm the worst.
I deserve this.
How can I change so that you'll like me?
What did I do wrong?"

You string me along,
cutting the line when the game became boring.
I tried to give you everything,
You said no thank you.
I would have stolen more for you
But it's never been about the value of my offerings,
It's what my value means to you.

I wasn't good enough for you.
I should have never let myself feel so fucking sorry.
I'm unapologetic, I'm healed,
And I am done being something created just for you to play
with.

I forgot, briefly, what I made myself into;
I forgot what I've been through,
The suffering, the work, the effort.
You make me forget who I am.

So I'm done pretending.
You no longer have control over me,
You will not make the decision to throw me away, you don't
have the power.

You fucked up.
If you want this fixed,
Go ahead and start.
Because I'm done trying.

Thinking Of You, Until The Very End

As similarly to death, to cause a revelation,
Orgasms result in epiphanies.
Rising action is much of the same as a series of trials
resulting in wisdom,
Images of you in my brain flood like prayers.

And within that blissful rest,
After the revelation,
I find myself still learning-

About you, about myself,
Of the world which I gladly stand beneath,
And hold in my broken fingers.

You, the sun who blinds me,
A deity I cannot part my attention from
Not for the smallest moment,
Lest I miss even one second of the shining of your rays.

And if you are the moon,
I will praise you in the wilderness,
Naked and blasphemous,
All for the sake
Of epiphany.

Timeless Retrograde

Every second with you is torture
Each second in passing can never be revived
So every second is agony
Because soon time will resume
And once more our feet will be dragged down to earth
The surface must catch us, and halt our hidden time warp
Then time will resume
And the seconds we spent together
Will only exist inside us.

Every second without you is torture
I am reminded constantly about you
I see you face in the empty air around me
Your lips stained my own, and I'll never get rid of the taste
Agony is in the anticipation
The longing is the dreaded existence which binds us
So wrongfully grounded.

Until we may meet again, I will sustain my existence by
wallowing in this torment
I breath in the disgusting air which isn't from your own
mouth
I'll walk the planet as if I haven't lived in the stars
Time will go on, restlessly consuming us all slowly
But life will halt
We will keep growing older with every day
But the devastation of our departure will not heal
The open wound of longing keeps us bleeding
And I will continuously pick the scab
So that I may remember the wonderful pain I keep
experiencing.

Trauma In A Coffee Shop

"Your butt's getting so big,"

He did it right in front of you.
You reprimanded him,
But took no action.

If only to further the fact you knew,
You always did,
And still did nothing.

At the time, I was thankful you said something,
Anything at all to douse the putrid flames he set in my
intestines.
Don't you know feeding flames air only makes them stink
even more?

But I will never thank you again,

1. You didn't do anything

2. You never said anything else

3. You're dead now

Why am I thinking about this now?
I'm just trying to enjoy my breakfast.

Untitled Document

You make me want to sing out loud
Or scream
Both are equally preferable
And so utterly fantastic
To feel that urge
To make noise again
And forget the oppressive silence I've lived within for years.

Untitled Document (2)

The incessant need to fight off the end is as silly as the worship of idols,
When the stars are ashes and the ground is a sinkhole - they will be the only ones not laughing.

The street will line with the dead, doors acting as coffins, houses mass graves.
A sky burned blue long ago, a distant reflection of the blood which now drowns us all.

Vows

Inside the most devoted minds
Sits a little man on a hamster wheel.
If he falls,
Or runs to an exhaustive death,
He can no longer serve.

Picking a God is devastating,
And conforming to a devotee is just as wasteful;
And when that creator asks too much
We run and run and run until we drop.

Disappointing is worse than delivering to our own needs.
To find oneself not giving everything,
Even life perseveres,
Means you're not giving enough.

> *"It's not sufficient!*
> *Lay down your life in my name,*
> *So that I may have a stepping stone,*
> *Less my feet dirty.*
> *And I better not hear you screaming*
> *Before you drown."*

Wasted! Potential!

What am I doing?
What the fuck am I doing?

I've had years to let it all escape.
Time I've wasted, doing what?

Masturbating, distracting myself,
Fucking, crying, and feeling sorry for myself.

It's unfair, to myself,
What I've done.

A thousand screams still sound in my head,
It's not that I've silenced them, or maybe I've just gotten cloudy.

My biggest fear is blocking the damn,
Even if it kills me, even if I drown, I will never stop the ideas from coming.

Creating is pain,
And I need to hurt myself more.

I need to come close to killing myself, again,
Not all the way, just teasing myself enough to remember.

I don't remember what it feels like to be happy, don't be fucking melodramatic!

I just mean that now that I am I have no fucking clue what to do with myself.

So what am I doing? Writing sappy poetry?
How fucking sad.

I need to pick my pen back up,
And stab myself repeatedly until that ink bleeds beauty again.

Or I die.
Either way, I need to do something.

What The Fuck (kill your mom)

I always resort to the same temptation.
A yearning, of the worst kind.
To write poetry about killing my mother.

Something so fascinating, so tantalizing and interesting;
An idea many can relate to, be consumed by.

I wish for the people who mean only ill may express
themselves so that we get all the fucked up shit just without
the deaths.

Or screw it.
Kill your fucking mother.

No.

Don't actually.
I'm just bored.

Won't Last Forever

Don't smash your face into the wall.
Don't bludgeon your head onto the concrete, holding your own hair.

But I want to.
I want to.
I want to.

I hope my nose breaks
I want my face to look so bloody you forget who I am.
I've always been a shadow-
Now see me as I am.

Writing Poetry in a Club

City streets laugh, but the cold indoors warms my aching.
Free me, I want to die all over again.

I wish you were here, I understand why people drink and
dance till 5am.
It would be so much better than walking the quiet streets,
So painfully alone.
If you were here
I'd swing you around until we collapsed.
I've waited too long to get here,
And all I can think about is you.

I've finally found a place where I'm not scared to turn
around.
Exposing my back allows for vulnerability,
But here I'm alright with that.
I've never felt safer surrounded by men or so welcomed in
the strangestest of places.
After running my whole life
I've slammed into the prettiest wall.
I think I'd be ok staying here.

The naked, gay men on the walls kiss comfort into my
aching wounds.
I've cut myself to bleed creativity,
And you've danced it out of me
In a jive I didn't think I could follow the steps of.
Though I love the metal in my skin,
I love the ache in my feet even more.
Pour me another, I'm going in!

XXX OOO XXX

Tighten my corset,
Kiss my binder.

I want you to lick me everywhere,
And bite me just as much.

Tell me I'm pretty, tell me I'm a good girl,
Then please call me handsome.

I can never get enough of your skin against mine,
Even when it's too much, I'd rather die than stop.

I'm your girl, I'm your nobody,
But what's important,
Is that I'm yours.
I'm yours.
I'm yours.
I'm yours.

Xenotransplant

To justify death is to explain a joke,
Utterly worthless is that of a broken comedian
Who's tongue is swallowed, and is no longer awarded an
audience.
Death is just so funny, isn't it?
Human nature is to turn to laughter in the face of great
tragedy.
So why pretend?
Why do we act like it isn't fucking hilarious when a rapist
gets their brains painted against a prison wall?

Consume me, find out, learn that the architecture of mental
illness is fine like silk, and tastes of rotten honey.
My   greatest   desire   is   to   be   eaten   alive.
My corpse will be more important than my living actions
ever could amend to.
So go ahead, have a taste.

What if I do kill myself?
Wouldn't that just be so selfish,
To deny another from that satisfaction?

I yearn for death like an orgasm that has been delayed to
the lifespan of an immortal.
Oh, I have had such delightful taste tests,
But none shall amount to the full course, I am assured of that.
She's visited me many, many times,
But as it goes I am yet still denied that last ending I seek
so dearly.

I grind my teeth to dust,
And pound my walls till my fingers break.
I eat my skin, and reveal in the taste of my insides.
If I could eat my tail as a snake just might,
Maybe then I would finally feel satisfied.

You Can't Possibly Be Real

I still can not fathom a reality where we both exist like this.
How could this ever be real?
This insatiable happiness, is so overwhelming;
I don't understand why it hurts so much
Just to think about you.

I close my eyes at night and you're the last thing I think of;
Mornings are indistinguishable, but not since you.
The morning rises and kisses dirty thoughts into my brain;
As soon as it starts, my eyes open and my heart beats too
hard.

The definite infinity of this existence halts at the quality
of you,
Shinning lines which burn my eyes burst into the sky and
consume the stars and sun.
As wicked as the moon, and as dangerous as the tides she
bores:
This world would mean nothing without your model
kindness, one which you cannot force.

How you exist is beyond my comprehension;
Why any God would bless me with this intertwined path, I
will forever be grateful despite my spite.
Every second we spend apart is agony,
And every moment I'm in your arms is far worse.

You hurt me in the most wonderful way,
It's exactly what I want
And exactly what I need.
I've never let anyone know me, not in the way I've opened
up to you.

You'll Always Have Me

My heart was ripped from my chest
And you hold it.

But I must always remind myself why I'm here.

Giving up would be so unhelpful,
I cannot express how stupid it be if I were to quit now.

Yes, I've found the love of my life.
Yes, it hurts so incredibly much to breathe without her.

No, I can't give up.

I want to pack up all my shit,
And quit, and see her.

But what then?

I'd be happy, and I could be with her,
But it would warrant my life useless.

Everything I've worked for my entire life would no longer
matter.

Every fight I'd be through, those mountains I'd dug through,
Would just be useless holes.

All that I've achieved cannot be forgotten, not even for love.

Not for the greatest love I've ever known, not even then,
May I give up on my future.

Zealous, Still Jealous

I like where I am,
In life,
In location.
I love this city, and what it's doing to me.

But I miss you.
More than conceivable,
More than what's even remotely fair.

I'm jealous of the air around you,
For it gets to touch you
And be in your presence.

I'm zealous in the path I'm on,
I love learning
In a way, I haven't felt in a very long time.

But I can't help missing you.
I cannot help thinking about you every second of every day.
Even laughing, talking, and amused, you're still the only
clear thought in my head.

I love you,
And I think I very well may love myself.

Printed in the United States
by Baker & Taylor Publisher Services